M4 iMac

Breaking Down Apple's Hidden Moves

A Deep Dive into Game-Changing Specs, Shifts, and What They Mean for You

Joe E. Grayson

Copyright © 2024 Joe E. Grayson, All rights reserved.

No part of this publication may be reproduced, distributed, or transmitted in any form or by any means, including photocopying, recording, or other electronic or mechanical methods, without the prior written permission of the publisher, except in the case of brief quotations embodied in critical reviews and certain other noncommercial uses permitted by copyright law.

Table of Contents

Introduction: The Silent Shift in Apple's Strategy

Chapter 1: The Evolution of the iMac Design

Chapter 2: The M4 Chip – Power Redefined

Chapter 3: Redefining User Experience with Memory and Storage

Chapter 4: Enhancing Connectivity with Thunderbolt Ports

Chapter 5: A New Look at Camera Technology

Chapter 6: Display Capabilities and the 8K Frontier

Chapter 7: Accessory Upgrades and the End of Lightning

Chapter 8: Display Glass Options and the Glare-Free Experience

Chapter 9: Practical Buying Advice and Configuration Tips

Chapter 10: Looking Ahead – How the M4 iMac Signals Apple's Future

Conclusion: The Impact of the M4 iMac on Today's Tech Landscape

Introduction: The Silent Shift in Apple's Strategy

Apple has always had a knack for keeping its audience captivated, often through grand reveals and carefully orchestrated events that transform product launches into cultural moments. However, recent announcements have seen Apple breaking away from the traditional stage, choosing quieter releases that shift the spotlight toward the products themselves rather than the presentation. This silent approach brings a new layer of intrigue, especially with the introduction of the M4 iMac. By opting out of its iconic event format, Apple allows the technology to speak for itself, a move that signals more than a simple shift in marketing. It hints at an evolution in

Apple's strategy—one that's more focused on the product's impact in users' daily lives rather than the pageantry of a launch.

The M4 iMac, nestled comfortably within Apple's current lineup, represents a carefully measured leap forward. Unlike the groundbreaking redesign of the M1 iMac or the incremental performance boosts of the M2 and M3 generations, the M4 iMac seems to have hit a sweet spot in Apple's vision. Its entry into the market was unannounced, yet it resonates with an understated power, adding notable enhancements to an already beloved model while staying rooted in the aesthetic and functional values that define the iMac family. This approach—quiet yet impactful—speaks volumes about Apple's confidence in its product evolution. They are no longer in a rush to reinvent; instead, they are refining, perfecting, and subtly raising the bar for users who seek seamless computing power wrapped in a visually compelling package.

In essence, the M4 iMac has come not with a fanfare but with a whisper of elegance and power, redefining the iMac experience in significant ways. This silent reveal does more than highlight Apple's subtle evolution; it marks a shift in how they engage with their audience. Each specification, from performance to connectivity, has been engineered with purpose, signaling that this is a machine not just for today but for the future—a device that hints at Apple's long-term vision for both desktop computing and user expectations.

The M4 iMac introduces a blend of high performance, refined design, and enhanced connectivity options, underscoring the themes

Apple continues to champion. Performance gains from the new M4 chip elevate its capabilities, placing it as a powerful yet accessible option for both casual and professional users. The design, while familiar, offers subtle enhancements that breathe new life into the device without straying from its iconic aesthetic. Connectivity has also taken a significant leap, reinforcing Apple's commitment to creating devices that not only operate as standalone machines but also integrate seamlessly within a larger ecosystem.

This quiet launch is also a promise—a hint that Apple is mapping out the future of computing in ways that may not always rely on spectacle but will consistently push the boundaries of technology. The M4 iMac is more than a product; it's a vision, a symbol of the silent shift in Apple's strategy, and a testament to their approach to innovation: not always loud but always impactful.

Chapter 1: The Evolution of the iMac Design

Apple's iMac has always been a canvas on which design and technology meet, capturing the spirit of its time while maintaining an elegance that is unmistakably Apple. The iMac's journey began with its 1998 debut—a bold, translucent shell in "Bondi Blue" that was unlike anything seen in computer design. Steve Jobs wanted to redefine not just how people used technology but how they felt about it. The iMac was never meant to be an impersonal machine; it was meant to engage, to become part of a user's world in a tangible way. Over the years, Apple continued to experiment with color, shape, and form, shifting from the original CRT to LCD screens and embracing increasingly minimalist designs with each generation. With each update, the iMac's silhouette became thinner, its borders more refined, stripping away what was unnecessary and leaving only the essence of a computer that felt both functional and artful.

In its latest iteration, the M4 iMac, Apple continues to honor this heritage of design. The 24-inch all-in-one form factor remains, a tribute to the balance of power and simplicity that defines the iMac. Rather than opting for a complete overhaul, Apple has chosen to refine, preserving a design that has proven itself to be efficient, sleek, and instantly recognizable. This all-in-one approach emphasizes ease and accessibility; there are no separate towers, no tangle of wires—a single, unified unit that's as much a part of the room as it is a powerful computing device. The decision to keep the 24-inch size speaks to Apple's understanding of spatial balance and visual harmony. This screen size strikes an ideal balance, large enough for creative projects and multitasking yet compact enough to fit comfortably in most workspaces.

One of the most exciting elements in this evolution is the refreshed color palette. Apple has taken a bold yet carefully calculated approach to color, giving each hue a slight twist, a fresh shade that feels both familiar and new. Beyond the typical silver, Apple has introduced shades that range from calming blues to a playful pink, a sunny yellow, and a natural green. These colors are not only beautiful but serve a deeper purpose: they are carefully chosen to evoke specific emotions and appeal to diverse personalities. Apple understands that users want a device that resonates with them on a personal level, and with this color variety, the iMac becomes more than just a computer—it's a statement piece. These choices subtly alter the relationship between the user and the product, making the iMac feel more like an extension of one's environment and personality.

For those who prefer a more understated look, silver is still available. But with these colors, Apple is signaling a shift away from its once monochromatic palette, a nod to its willingness to embrace variety and break out of its more traditional image. Moving beyond silver reflects an evolution in Apple's brand identity. Apple is tapping into a sense of individualism, recognizing that technology doesn't have to be sterile or solely functional; it can be vibrant, approachable, and designed to fit seamlessly into a user's life and style. This color strategy goes beyond aesthetics—it's a message that Apple products are meant to be as unique as the individuals who use them.

In essence, the iMac's design has become more than the sum of its parts. It's a celebration of form and function, a testament to Apple's deep understanding of design psychology, and a reflection of the shifting landscape of user expectations. The iMac is not just a device; it's a piece of art, an embodiment of the Apple ethos, and a glimpse into the future of technology where beauty, functionality, and individuality converge.

Chapter 2: The M4 Chip – Power Redefined

The M4 chip represents a new milestone in Apple's relentless pursuit of performance excellence, building upon the successes of the M1 and M3 with a series of impressive advancements. Designed around an advanced architecture, the M4 brings a refined balance between speed, efficiency, and adaptability, enabling the iMac to handle an even wider range of tasks. Apple's shift to proprietary silicon has always been about more than performance—it's about creating hardware that aligns seamlessly with its software ecosystem. With each generation, from the initial groundbreaking M1 to the more refined M3, Apple has demonstrated how in-house chip design enables tighter integration and efficiency. Now, with the M4, the iMac achieves a new level of power and versatility, setting it apart in a competitive landscape.

One of the most attention-grabbing figures in the M4 chip's specifications is the 1.7x performance increase over its predecessor. This boost isn't just a number for the sake of bragging rights; it's a quantifiable leap that has real implications for users. This increase in processing speed and graphical capability means that users can expect noticeably faster response times and smoother multitasking. Tasks that once required more patience, such as photo and video editing, rendering, or even complex spreadsheets, are now handled with impressive ease. The GPU improvements translate to better graphics processing, making the M4 iMac a capable machine for content creators, designers, and gamers alike. Animation, editing, and rendering are now smoother, and the transition between high-load applications feels effortless, creating a seamless user experience that was once reserved for high-end workstations.

For everyday users, this performance upgrade translates into an effortless experience for daily activities and multitasking. A student can switch between writing papers, browsing the web, and running data-heavy applications without the slightest lag. A creative professional might find the iMac's capability to handle large files and memory-intensive programs like Photoshop or Final Cut Pro more efficiently, allowing them to focus on the creative process rather than technical constraints. Even complex tasks like 3D modeling or working with AI-driven applications are well within the M4's capabilities, making it a versatile choice for both personal and professional settings.

In the context of the larger tech landscape, the M4 chip's release signals a bold move for Apple. The chip's performance rivals and, in many cases, surpasses competing processors, demonstrating Apple's commitment to pushing boundaries. Unlike traditional CPU/GPU setups found in other desktops, the M4 integrates Apple's silicon architecture with its operating system, enabling optimizations that aren't possible on non-Apple platforms. This allows Apple to continue refining macOS to take full advantage of the chip's unique capabilities, creating an ecosystem where software and hardware enhance each other's strengths. The performance of the M4 places Apple ahead in the race for powerful yet efficient personal computing, reshaping expectations for what an all-in-one desktop can deliver.

Apple's M4 chip goes beyond just raw power—it redefines what is possible in a user-focused desktop computer. It showcases Apple's commitment to delivering performance without sacrificing efficiency, enhancing every aspect of the user experience, from speed and responsiveness to graphics and productivity. This isn't just an upgrade; it's a glimpse into Apple's future direction, where cutting-edge performance is seamlessly woven into intuitive, elegantly designed devices that make powerful computing accessible to everyone. The M4 iMac isn't merely faster—it's an example of how Apple's vision for the future of computing is already becoming a reality.

Chapter 3: Redefining User Experience with Memory and Storage

The decision to make 16GB of RAM standard on the M4 iMac is a testament to Apple's understanding of user needs in a world where multitasking and memory-intensive applications have become the norm. For years, 8GB of RAM was the starting point for most entry-level machines, sufficient for light tasks but often limited when it came to heavy workflows or multitasking. By doubling the base memory to 16GB, Apple has created a machine that is better equipped for both everyday users and those who need more from their desktops. This move brings the iMac in line with the needs of today's digital landscape, allowing users to work smoothly across multiple applications, handle larger files, and perform resource-heavy tasks without the constraints they might have encountered with lower memory.

For power users, the shift to 16GB as the baseline means that they can now rely on a standard iMac configuration to meet most of their needs without constantly monitoring memory usage or fearing that an intensive application might slow down their workflow. Designers, developers, and professionals working in media production, for example, will find the extra memory particularly beneficial for projects that require handling large files or running demanding software. On the other hand, casual users—those who primarily browse the web, watch videos, and use office applications—may not notice as dramatic a change in daily performance, but the additional memory provides an extra layer of efficiency and future-proofing, ensuring that the iMac remains responsive and versatile as software demands grow.

When it comes to storage, Apple has kept the base model at 256GB, a choice that caters to casual users who rely on cloud storage or don't require extensive local storage. For those with basic needs, this amount can be perfectly adequate, especially when combined with Apple's integration with iCloud. Storing photos, documents, and essential files in the cloud frees up space on the device itself, creating a streamlined experience. However, for users who work with large files or manage a lot of media content—such as photos, videos, or design assets—an upgrade to a larger storage option, like 512GB or even 1TB, becomes more than just a convenience; it's essential.

Users planning to keep their iMac for several years might find the investment in additional storage worthwhile, especially given the growing file sizes of applications, operating system updates, and media. In creative fields or professional settings, where high-resolution images, video footage, and design files can quickly accumulate, 256GB may feel restrictive over time. Moving to a 512GB or 1TB configuration not only ensures sufficient space for work projects and media collections but also reduces the need to constantly manage and offload files to external storage, making for a more seamless, all-in-one experience.

Ultimately, the configuration choices on the M4 iMac reflect Apple's intent to serve a broad user base, from casual users who appreciate simplicity and speed to professionals who require more power and flexibility. By standardizing 16GB of RAM, Apple has taken a definitive step toward a more versatile machine, catering to those who need both performance and convenience. Meanwhile, the storage options allow users to tailor their iMac to their specific needs and ensure that it remains a capable companion for years to come. With this setup, Apple has designed the M4 iMac to offer both immediate ease of use and the longevity needed to keep up with the evolving demands of modern computing, redefining what users can expect from a base-level desktop experience.

Chapter 4: Enhancing Connectivity with Thunderbolt Ports

Apple's journey with connectivity has always been about leading users into new eras of speed, efficiency, and versatility. Early on, Apple embraced USB technology, introducing it as a standard across its devices. As demands for faster data transfer and higher-quality media support grew, Apple adopted the Thunderbolt standard, a technology it helped pioneer with Intel. With each iteration of Thunderbolt, users gained an exponential boost in connectivity, enabling seamless connections between devices, faster data transfer, and support for high-resolution external displays. This evolution reflects Apple's commitment to providing users with tools that are as efficient as they are forward-looking, making each connection point more powerful and versatile with every upgrade.

On the M4 iMac, Apple has gone a step further by expanding its Thunderbolt ports to four on higher-end models, a feature that enhances productivity and flexibility for users who rely on multiple peripherals and external devices. This expanded port selection offers a significant increase in input/output capacity, allowing users to connect additional displays, storage devices, and accessories without needing adapters or hubs. With four Thunderbolt ports, users can create a fully integrated workstation, capable of supporting dual 4K displays or even an 8K display, high-speed external storage, audio interfaces, and other high-performance devices simultaneously. For professionals who depend on rapid data transfer and seamless connectivity, this array of ports transforms the iMac from a standard desktop into a highly customizable productivity hub.

Looking beyond the iMac, the addition of four Thunderbolt ports might be a sign of what's to come across Apple's product lineup. There are already indications that future MacBook Pro models and even a potential M4 Mac Mini could adopt similar configurations, allowing users in various environments to benefit from enhanced connectivity. As Thunderbolt 4 technology becomes more integrated across Apple's range, the potential for advanced, interconnected workstations grows. This approach aligns with Apple's ecosystem philosophy, where devices are optimized to work seamlessly with one another. It's plausible that future iterations of Thunderbolt on Apple devices will bring even faster data transfer rates, support for more displays, and higher power delivery, furthering the utility of the Thunderbolt standard as a unifying feature across Apple products.

In practice, the four Thunderbolt ports on the M4 iMac open up a world of possibilities for diverse user scenarios. Creative professionals, for example, might use one port for an external display, another for a high-speed external SSD, and still have ports available for a digital audio interface or graphics tablet. Video editors can connect multiple 4K or even 8K displays, streamlining the editing process by enhancing visual clarity and screen space. For those who handle large media files, the high-speed data transfer enabled by Thunderbolt allows for rapid file transfers between external drives and the iMac, saving valuable time in data-heavy workflows. Even casual users can benefit, with options to easily connect their iMac to multiple devices without hassle, whether it's a second display for multitasking or peripherals for a better multimedia experience.

In essence, Apple's expansion of Thunderbolt ports on the M4 iMac does more than add connectivity options; it redefines the iMac's role in a modern workspace. This enhancement shows Apple's commitment to flexibility and performance, catering to a user base that increasingly demands versatile and reliable ways to connect and create. The integration of four Thunderbolt ports reflects Apple's understanding of how people work today, supporting a range of configurations that suit different needs while laying the groundwork for an Apple ecosystem built on speed, efficiency, and the power of seamless connectivity.

Chapter 5: A New Look at Camera Technology

Apple's integration of the Center Stage camera on the M4 iMac represents a thoughtful upgrade aimed at enhancing the user experience in video calls, meetings, and virtual gatherings. Unlike a standard webcam, the Center Stage camera utilizes an ultrawide lens to track and adjust the frame as users move, ensuring they stay centered even if they shift positions or share the frame with others. This tracking capability, a feature first introduced on the iPad, brings a new level of dynamism to video calls, particularly for FaceTime and conferencing applications. The result is a more engaging experience, as the camera's subtle adjustments create a natural, almost conversational flow that feels closer to in-person interactions.

However, the benefits of the ultrawide field of view come with certain trade-offs, most notably in terms of resolution. The Center Stage feature relies on cropping the ultrawide image to maintain the subject in the frame, which can lead to a reduction in clarity compared to previous iMac models equipped with a high-resolution 1080p camera. While this difference may be noticeable to users accustomed to the sharpness of previous models, it's a reasonable trade-off for those who prioritize the flexibility of a camera that adapts to movement and multiple people. The camera technology is designed to balance resolution with functionality, ensuring that users still enjoy high video quality while benefiting from the camera's ability to follow them naturally within the frame.

In everyday life, the usability of the Center Stage camera shines in a variety of scenarios. For users working from home or attending virtual classes, the camera's tracking ability allows them to move freely within their workspace without worrying about staying perfectly centered in the shot. This is particularly useful for presenters, instructors, or anyone who gestures or moves while speaking. For families or groups sharing the same device for video calls, the Center Stage camera keeps everyone visible and centered, adding a layer of convenience and engagement that a static camera simply can't provide. This adaptability makes the M4 iMac a valuable tool for modern digital communication, where flexibility and ease of use are paramount.

Looking forward, the introduction of Center Stage on the iMac could be a glimpse into Apple's future plans for camera technology across its devices. The success of this feature on the iMac might pave the way for similar functionality in other Apple products, including MacBook Pros and even desktop monitors. As Apple refines this technology, we may see improvements in how the camera balances resolution with tracking, possibly using advanced sensors or software enhancements to deliver even sharper video quality without sacrificing the ultrawide tracking capability. This shift points to a future where Apple's devices are increasingly optimized for virtual interaction, responding to the growing demand for seamless, high-quality video communication across professional, educational, and personal contexts.

In essence, the Center Stage camera on the M4 iMac embodies Apple's commitment to blending technology with practical, human-centered design. This feature goes beyond novelty; it represents a shift in how Apple views the role of webcams in an era of constant connectivity. With Center Stage, Apple is not just enhancing video quality; it's redefining the video call experience, making it more dynamic, intuitive, and adaptable to the realities of today's digital interactions.

Chapter 6: Display Capabilities and the 8K Frontier

The M4 iMac introduces an unprecedented capability: the power to drive an external 8K display at 120Hz. This feature marks a new chapter in desktop display technology, setting Apple's iMac apart by catering to the high-performance needs of professionals and creatives. In practical terms, an 8K display operating at 120Hz offers a visual experience that's almost unmatched, with crystal-clear resolution, heightened color depth, and a refresh rate that ensures smooth motion and responsiveness. For tasks like video editing, 3D rendering, or even high-end gaming, this capability delivers an unparalleled level of detail and fluidity, setting a new benchmark in display performance and expanding the creative possibilities for users.

The inclusion of 8K support on the iMac begs the question: why now? Apple has always been strategic in timing its technology releases, often holding back until there's a clear, practical advantage for users. The choice to support 8K resolution at this moment suggests that Apple is preparing for the next wave of professional and creative demands. Content creators are increasingly working with 4K and even 8K footage, making high-resolution displays an essential tool for accurate editing and grading. For Apple, integrating 8K support aligns with a larger vision of enabling creators to work at the highest level of quality, preparing them for a future where ultra-high-resolution content is not just desirable but necessary.

At the heart of this new capability lies the M4 chip's upgraded display driver. This enhanced driver allows the iMac to manage high-resolution data at the kind of speed and efficiency required for 8K output. This level of display capability means that users don't just have a powerful machine in terms of processing and memory but also a device that can support future advancements in display technology. By introducing this feature now, Apple ensures that the iMac will remain relevant as 8K displays become more accessible, effectively future-proofing the device for users who want to maximize its lifespan and utility.

The addition of 8K compatibility also hints at Apple's potential expansion of its Pro Display lineup. The current Pro Display XDR, while celebrated for its exceptional 6K resolution and HDR capabilities, might soon be joined by an 8K sibling. This could bring a whole new level of visual clarity and responsiveness to Apple's display offerings, catering specifically to professionals in fields like film production, animation, and photography who require both high resolution and high refresh rates for their workflows. An 8K Pro Display would position Apple as a leader in professional-grade monitors, attracting users who need absolute precision and immersion in their visual workspaces.

In sum, the M4 iMac's 8K support is not just a spec to boast about; it's a forward-thinking feature that anticipates the needs of a growing professional market. Apple's investment in high-resolution, high-refresh displays underscores its commitment to leading the industry in display technology and providing tools that empower creators to realize their visions with unparalleled accuracy and detail. By integrating 8K capabilities into the iMac, Apple isn't merely enhancing the desktop experience—it's laying the foundation for the next generation of visual excellence.

Chapter 7: Accessory Upgrades and the End of Lightning

Apple's decision to transition from Lightning to USB-C across its devices reflects a long-anticipated alignment with universal charging standards and user demands. The move to USB-C isn't just a technical update; it's a response to the growing expectation for compatibility and convenience. With USB-C now the standard for Apple's latest iMac accessories—the Magic Keyboard, Trackpad, and Mouse—users benefit from a streamlined ecosystem, allowing them to use a single cable across multiple devices. USB-C integration simplifies the user experience, particularly for those invested in multiple Apple products, reducing the need for proprietary cables and making Apple's lineup more accessible and versatile.

The upgrade of the Magic accessories to include USB-C is a small yet significant step in Apple's push toward standardization. The Magic Keyboard and Trackpad now charge via USB-C, making them more adaptable to Apple's evolving ecosystem. For users, this update means faster charging and easier compatibility across Apple's lineup, from Macs to iPads, ensuring that they have fewer cables to manage and a more efficient charging experience overall. These accessories have long been celebrated for their sleek design and seamless integration with Apple devices, and this update only reinforces their reputation as indispensable parts of the iMac experience.

However, one design choice continues to draw mixed reactions: the charging port on the Magic

Mouse remains on the underside of the device. This placement, a point of debate since its introduction, requires users to flip the mouse over to charge, rendering it unusable during charging. For many, this design choice feels counterintuitive, particularly given Apple's history of prioritizing user-centered design. However, Apple's rationale may lie in aesthetics and simplicity—keeping the mouse's surface clean and uninterrupted, a choice that aligns with Apple's minimalistic design philosophy. For users who rely heavily on the Magic Mouse, this quirk may be an inconvenience, but given the device's quick-charging capability, Apple likely considers this compromise acceptable within its design language.

Public response to these accessory updates has been mixed, reflecting a blend of appreciation and critique that often accompanies Apple's design choices. The shift to USB-C has been widely applauded, seen as a long-overdue move that aligns with industry standards and meets user expectations for convenience. However, the Magic Mouse port placement remains polarizing, with some users frustrated by the persistent inconvenience, while others accept it as a minor issue in an otherwise well-designed device. Apple's approach here showcases its tendency to balance user feedback with its own vision, sometimes prioritizing design coherence over practicality, trusting that users will adapt to the quirks in exchange for a device that looks and feels distinctly Apple.

In essence, the accessory updates on the M4 iMac embody Apple's ongoing commitment to refinement and uniformity. The transition to USB-C brings Apple closer to the seamless, interconnected experience it envisions for its users, while the continued design quirks remind us of Apple's unique approach to product design. The shift represents a thoughtful evolution, one that honors user expectations while retaining the signature look and feel that Apple is known for. Through these updates, Apple reinforces its brand identity—innovative yet consistent, user-focused yet artistically uncompromising.

Chapter 8: Display Glass Options and the Glare-Free Experience

Apple's introduction of the nano-textured glass option on the M4 iMac is a thoughtful enhancement aimed at users who require an optimized viewing experience, particularly in spaces with challenging lighting conditions. For an additional $200, this option allows users to reduce screen glare significantly, ensuring that reflections or harsh lighting don't interfere with clarity or color accuracy. The nano-textured glass is engineered to scatter light across the surface of the display, eliminating most of the glare while preserving contrast and sharpness. It's a subtle but powerful improvement that allows users to work comfortably in environments with natural or artificial light, from bright offices to studios with large windows, providing a more immersive and undisturbed viewing experience.

This feature is particularly suited for professionals who rely on precise visual details and color accuracy, making it an attractive option for creative fields like photography, design, and video editing. In these industries, screen visibility is crucial, as even minor glare can interfere with image quality and color assessment. For example, photographers editing high-resolution images or designers working on intricate details can benefit greatly from this anti-glare technology, as it minimizes the visual distractions that could affect their work. Even for general office use, where lighting conditions may change throughout the day, the nano-textured glass provides a comfortable viewing experience that can help reduce eye strain, ensuring that users remain focused and productive.

When deciding between the nano-textured glass and the standard glass, users should consider their typical work environment. The standard display works well in controlled lighting settings, delivering excellent clarity and contrast at a lower cost. However, for those who frequently work in variable or brightly lit spaces, the nano-textured glass offers a distinct advantage. It not only enhances visibility in direct light but also preserves color integrity, which can be compromised by screen reflections on standard glass. For users who rely on visual precision, the nano-textured option becomes a valuable investment, allowing them to work confidently without needing to adjust their environment constantly.

This feature is also a strategic addition to Apple's professional market offerings, reinforcing its commitment to creating devices that cater to specialized needs. By including the nano-textured glass option, Apple positions the iMac as a versatile tool for diverse work environments, from design studios to open-plan offices. The availability of this upgrade broadens the iMac's appeal to professionals who might otherwise look to external monitors or other workarounds to address glare issues. In doing so, Apple strengthens its presence in the professional market, providing solutions that are not only visually effective but seamlessly integrated into the iMac's sleek design.

The nano-textured glass option on the M4 iMac exemplifies Apple's dedication to offering practical, high-quality solutions for real-world challenges. It is an upgrade that elevates the iMac's adaptability in varied lighting conditions, ensuring that it meets the demands of users who prioritize an optimal visual experience. Through this feature, Apple demonstrates its understanding of the professional environment, offering a nuanced solution that enhances productivity, comfort, and visual accuracy in a variety of settings.

Chapter 9: Practical Buying Advice and Configuration Tips

Choosing the right M4 iMac configuration can be a pivotal decision, with options designed to cater to both casual users and professionals seeking a powerful, long-lasting desktop. Apple's lineup for the M4 iMac typically offers a base model, a mid-tier model, and a top-tier model, each with different levels of performance, storage, and connectivity options. The base model provides a well-rounded experience for users with standard computing needs, while the mid-tier and top-tier configurations introduce added performance and flexibility, particularly beneficial for users who handle more demanding workflows.

The base model is equipped with 16GB of RAM and 256GB of storage, making it ideal for those who primarily use the iMac for everyday tasks such as web browsing, document editing, and streaming. This model provides ample memory for multitasking and a smooth experience in most standard applications. However, users who work with larger files, or who expect their storage needs to grow, may find the 256GB limit restrictive over time. For these users, upgrading to the mid-tier model, which includes 512GB of storage and additional Thunderbolt ports, offers a comfortable balance between affordability and enhanced performance.

For those looking to future-proof their iMac, opting for the mid-tier or top-tier model with storage upgrades can be a wise choice. Investing in 512GB or even 1TB of storage allows for more flexibility, ensuring that users have the capacity to store large media files, applications, and projects without immediately needing external storage. Moreover, the mid-tier and top-tier configurations often come with four Thunderbolt ports, which enhance connectivity and make the iMac a more versatile option in environments where multiple peripherals, such as external displays or high-speed storage, are required. By choosing one of these configurations, users can enjoy a longer lifespan for their iMac, knowing it can keep up with evolving software and storage demands.

Understanding how each configuration suits different user needs is crucial in maximizing the iMac's value. For casual users—those who spend most of their time browsing, streaming, and working on basic office tasks—the base model provides all the essential functionality at a competitive price. It offers enough power and memory to handle daily activities without feeling over-engineered for light use. However, power users, including creatives, developers, and professionals handling data-intensive tasks, may benefit from higher configurations. The extra memory and storage in the mid and top-tier models provide the support needed for applications like photo editing, video rendering, and software development, where more power and space can dramatically improve productivity.

When considering a configuration for longevity, it's worth evaluating how your needs might change over the years. Opting for 16GB of memory is a solid choice across all models, as it accommodates most users' needs and offers room for future software demands. However, upgrading storage at the outset is a smart investment for those expecting to work with large files or extensive media libraries. For users in creative industries or technical fields, the top-tier model with 1TB storage and maximum port options may be the best choice, allowing for a high-performance setup that remains flexible as projects grow more complex.

In summary, the best configuration for each user will depend on their current and anticipated needs. The M4 iMac's varied configurations are designed to offer a tailored experience, whether you're a casual user seeking simplicity or a professional looking to maximize performance and longevity. Apple's range of options empowers users to choose a setup that not only meets today's requirements but also remains reliable and efficient well into the future. This thoughtful approach to customization ensures that every user, from the occasional web surfer to the seasoned creative, can find a model that's uniquely suited to their goals and workflow.

Chapter 10: Looking Ahead – How the M4 iMac Signals Apple's Future

The release of the M4 iMac provides more than just a glimpse into Apple's immediate advancements; it reveals key aspects of Apple's long-term strategy for its ecosystem. This iMac, with its mix of performance, design, and forward-looking features, represents Apple's approach to refining and future-proofing its products while responding to evolving user needs. Positioned as an all-in-one that is both powerful and approachable, the M4 iMac integrates effortlessly into Apple's lineup, complementing devices like the MacBook and iPad with the added capabilities of a high-performance desktop. Its role within Apple's ecosystem is clear: it is the central hub for users who seek a desktop experience with robust computing power, versatile connectivity, and seamless integration with other Apple devices.

The M4 iMac's design and feature set may also foreshadow developments across the rest of the Mac lineup. Speculation around potential releases like an M4 Mac Mini or M4 MacBook Pro suggests that Apple is committed to extending the power of the M4 chip across its devices, creating a cohesive suite of products that cater to a variety of computing needs. The rumored M4 Mac Mini, for instance, would offer desktop users a compact yet powerful alternative to the iMac, while the M4 MacBook Pro could bring portable, high-performance computing to those who require flexibility. By equipping these devices with the M4's enhanced capabilities, Apple strengthens its Mac lineup, providing options that are increasingly tailored to both consumer and professional demands. Each product would benefit from the M4 chip's efficient architecture, setting a new standard for performance across Apple's hardware.

The 8K display capabilities and expanded Thunderbolt ports on the M4 iMac indicate Apple's commitment to solidifying its position as a leader in pro computing and display technology. The ability to support 8K displays at 120Hz, a first for the iMac, suggests that Apple is not merely enhancing current capabilities but also preparing for what's next in high-resolution display technology. This aligns with Apple's strategy of appealing to professional users, particularly in fields that demand exceptional visual precision and clarity. By positioning the iMac as a machine that can handle the most advanced display requirements, Apple is expanding its appeal to industries that rely on detailed visual work, from video editing to 3D modeling. The adoption of multiple Thunderbolt ports further solidifies Apple's commitment to a versatile, interconnected workspace, reinforcing its dedication to an ecosystem that supports seamless integration and high-speed data exchange.

The staying power of the iMac's all-in-one design is also a testament to Apple's understanding of the role desktop computing plays in modern workspaces. While mobile devices like the MacBook and iPad have garnered attention for their portability, the iMac's enduring popularity shows that there is a distinct place for powerful, stationary computing. Apple has carefully evolved the iMac over the years, refining its form factor and functionality to meet contemporary expectations. The M4 iMac's release reaffirms

Apple's belief in the all-in-one concept, where performance, design, and connectivity converge in a single, self-contained unit. This design philosophy allows the iMac to serve as an anchor in a digital workspace, providing users with a consistent, powerful, and aesthetically pleasing device that integrates seamlessly into their workflow.

Looking ahead, the M4 iMac signals Apple's dedication to creating products that are adaptable to future demands. By investing in advanced chip architecture, high-resolution display compatibility, and robust connectivity, Apple positions the iMac—and, by extension, its entire Mac lineup—as the core of its pro-focused offerings. This forward-thinking approach not only keeps Apple at the forefront of computing technology but also caters to a wide range of users, from everyday consumers to industry professionals. In doing so, Apple continues to shape the future of all-in-one computing, blending power and elegance in ways that enhance both productivity and creativity, and redefining what users can expect from their desktops in a rapidly evolving tech landscape.

Conclusion: The Impact of the M4 iMac on Today's Tech Landscape

The M4 iMac represents a defining moment in Apple's lineup, blending powerful new capabilities with refined design choices that set a high standard for the future of all-in-one computing. At its core, the M4 iMac introduces a host of key features that elevate its performance, connectivity, and user experience. The M4 chip, with its 1.7x performance boost over previous models, delivers a seamless, responsive experience, whether for creative workflows or everyday multitasking. Enhanced connectivity with up to four Thunderbolt ports expands its utility as a versatile hub, supporting everything from high-speed data transfer to 8K external displays. And with Apple's decision to offer nano-textured glass, users in bright or variable lighting environments now have an option to work comfortably with minimal glare. These carefully crafted features underscore Apple's commitment to making the iMac a powerful, adaptable, and future-ready machine.

In many ways, the M4 iMac serves as a testament to Apple's lasting influence on the tech landscape and its ability to shape consumer expectations. The iMac's enduring appeal lies in its ability to balance high performance with elegant design, making cutting-edge technology approachable to a wide audience. By transitioning to a 16GB RAM baseline and offering flexible storage options, Apple acknowledges the need for powerful, accessible desktops that cater to a diverse user base. The shift to USB-C across its accessories also demonstrates Apple's commitment to a streamlined, interconnected ecosystem that enhances convenience without sacrificing style. These changes reflect not only Apple's attention to user needs but also its influence on industry standards, setting benchmarks that often guide the tech world forward.

In a rapidly evolving tech world, Apple's strategic evolution of the iMac signals more than just an iterative update; it sets the stage for future industry trends. The subtle yet impactful upgrades to display capabilities, such as 8K support, position Apple as a leader in visual technology, appealing to creative professionals and power users alike. Additionally, the adoption of Thunderbolt 4 connectivity and the growing integration of Apple's ecosystem speak to a future where devices are more interconnected and adaptable, designed to handle the increasing demands of creative and professional workspaces. Apple's quiet but calculated approach with the M4 iMac release exemplifies a commitment to innovation that respects tradition while embracing the future, making the iMac not only a piece of hardware but also a symbol of forward-thinking design.

The journey of the M4 iMac is a story of evolution, refinement, and vision. It embodies Apple's core values of innovation, usability, and design excellence, inviting users to embrace its capabilities with confidence. The M4 iMac is more than a desktop—it's a reminder of how technology can seamlessly fit into our lives, enhancing productivity and creativity while staying true to Apple's legacy. For those considering the M4 iMac, this is a device built for both today and tomorrow, designed to support a wide range of needs with elegance and power. As Apple continues to chart the course of the tech industry, the M4 iMac stands as a testament to what a well-crafted, thoughtful approach to computing can achieve.

www.ingramcontent.com/pod-product-compliance
Lightning Source LLC
Chambersburg PA
CBHW070129230526
45472CB00004B/1488